Made in the USA
Las Vegas, NV
30 October 2023

79996121R00061